First World War
and Army of Occupation
War Diary
France, Belgium and Germany

28 DIVISION
Divisional Troops
1/1 Northumbrian Field Company Royal Engineers
and 2/1 Northumbrian Field Company Royal Engineers
18 January 1915 - 31 May 1915

WO95/2272/2-3

The Naval & Military Press Ltd
www.nmarchive.com
Published in association with The National Archives

Published by

The Naval & Military Press Ltd

Unit 10 Ridgewood Industrial Park,

Uckfield, East Sussex,

TN22 5QE England

Tel: +44 (0) 1825 749494

www.naval-military-press.com

www.nmarchive.com

This diary has been reprinted in facsimile from the original. Any imperfections are inevitably reproduced and the quality may fall short of modern type and cartographic standards.

© Crown Copyright
Images reproduced by permission of The National Archives, London, England, 2015.

Contents

Document type	Place/Title	Date From	Date To
Heading	WO95/2272/2		
Heading	28th Division Divl Engineers 1/1st Northumbrian Fld Coy R.E. Jan-May 1915 To 50 Division		
Heading	1st Northampton Field Coy. R.E. (28th Division) Vol I 18.1 4.3.15 Jan-Oct 15		
War Diary	Standon Camp Winchester	18/01/1915	18/01/1915
War Diary	Southampton	18/01/1915	18/01/1915
War Diary	Havre	19/01/1915	19/01/1915
War Diary	No. 2 Camp Havre	20/01/1915	21/01/1915
War Diary	Cassel	22/01/1915	22/01/1915
War Diary	Caestre	23/01/1915	02/02/1915
War Diary	Vlamertinghe	03/02/1915	08/02/1915
War Diary	Ypres	08/02/1915	04/03/1915
War Diary	Vlamertinghe	01/03/1915	12/03/1915
War Diary	Ypres	12/03/1915	25/03/1915
Heading	28th Division 1st Northern Train Field Coy R.E. Vol II 5.3-30.4.15		
War Diary	Ypres	05/03/1915	26/03/1915
War Diary	General	26/03/1915	18/04/1915
War Diary	Ypres	19/04/1915	30/04/1915
Heading	28th Division 1st Northern Train Field Coy R.E. Vol III 1-31.5.15		
War Diary	Ypres	01/05/1915	31/05/1915
Heading	WO95/2272/3		
Heading	BEF 28 Div Troops 2/1 Northumbrian Fld Coy RE 1915 Jly 1915 Oct To Salonika		
War Diary	England	03/07/1915	03/07/1915
War Diary	France Le Havre	04/07/1915	10/07/1915
War Diary	Kemmel	14/07/1915	30/09/1915
War Diary	Vermelles	01/10/1915	25/10/1915

WO95/2272(2)

WO95/2272(2)

1ST NORTHUMBRIAN FLD COY R.E.
JAN - MAY 1915

No Division to 50 Division

28TH DIVISION
DIVL ENGINEERS

121/4559

1st Northumbrian Field Coy: R.E. (28th Division).

Vol I.   18.1 —— 4.3.15

Jan — Oct '15

WAR DIARY or INTELLIGENCE SUMMARY

Army Form C. 2118.

Instructions regarding War Diaries and Intelligence Summaries are contained in F. S. Regs., Part II. and the Staff Manual respectively. Title pages will be prepared in manuscript.

1st Northumbrian Field Co. RE (Erase heading not required.)

Hour, Date, Place	Summary of Events and Information	Remarks and references to Appendices
Standon Camp. Winchester 18/1/15	Marched to Southampton & embarked on Bellerophon & Maidan. Left camp 10.30 a.m. reached docks 2.15 p.m. On Bellerophon: 5 Officers, 7 Sergeants, 2 Trumpeters, 6 Corporals, 6 II Corpls, 155 Sappers, 43 drivers = 224 15 Vehicles, 32 Bicycles On Maidan: 1 Sergeant, 8 drivers = 9 79 Horses Total all ranks 233 on board Add Advance party: AMLO Capt E.C. Burnup } at Havre 5" Stanger } Billetting party { Cpl Mitchell { II Cpl Lurgford } 4 = 237 In France In hospital - Hursley 1 Absent 1 = 2 239 Total strength	
Southampton 18/1/15 6 p.m. Havre 19/1/15	Left dock. Quiet passage. No casualties. Arrived about 5 a.m. docked about 12.30 p.m. Left docks for No.2 Rest camp about 7.30 p.m. reached camp 9 p.m. 2 Sappers (Crow & Howe) absent when we left dock.	W Bunney Capt M.O.O. 1st N.F.C. RE
No 2 Camp. Havre 20/1/15	Roll called 9 a.m. 2 absent. Strength 231 + 1 Interpreter = 232	
Do. 21/1/15	Left camp at 4.30 a.m. & entrained at Gare des marchandises. All present 234 + Capt Burnup = 235 + 79 horses.	

WARDIARY
or
INTELLIGENCE SUMMARY
(Erase heading not required.)

Army Form C. 2118.

Instructions regarding War Diaries and Intelligence Summaries are contained in F. S. Regs., Part II. and the Staff Manual respectively. Title pages will be prepared in manuscript.

Hour, Date, Place	Summary of Events and Information	Remarks and references to Appendices
Cassel 22/1/15	Arrived at 8 a.m. Detrained & marched to Caestre where we billeted in farm Reini Gresse. Posted of Cpls Mitchell & Lunsford.	1 Horse, 1 Interpreter
Caestre 23/1/15	Saw CRE at Steller. Standing by.	230 R&F. 79 horses
26/1/15 Tuesday	Rain & continuing storms. Wet night, cold. Heavy firing to Eastward on same line.	
" 27/1/15	Tried French Howitzer & Grenades.	
" 28/1/15	Reviewed by C in C. Lt Toole arrived on 30/1/15.	
" 2/2/15	Left Caestre at 7.30 a.m. & marched with 85 Bde to VLAMERTINGHE via Bailleul & Locre, arriving in billet at 5 p.m. No.1 Section (Lt Toole) with 85 Bde at Boeschepe.	
VLAMERTINGHE 3/2/15	Moved to new farm. Started on huts.	
" 4/2/15	Busy hutting. Rode to YPRES to try for stores. Heavy shell fire S. of YPRES.	
" 5/2/15	On huts. Visited trenches with Toole & White to inspect mine.	
" 8/2/15	Moved to YPRES. Billeted in Rue de Lombard. Working party in trenches at night. No. 1132 Sapper J B Gibbon wounded.	
YPRES	Spent whole of week 9/2/15 – 13/2/15 in trenches. No record kept of work done.	
" 11/2/15	Shell burst at door of billet & killed following:— No. 987 Sapper T. Graham 993 Dr A Luke 991 T/Sm J Wilson 104 RMS H Curtis (died 12/2/15) Five horses killed & 9.5 wagon & harness wrecked.	Wounded by same shell 767 Sapper G W Hardy 1599 D W Ferguson 1241 S E W T Padett

W Dunning Capt
p. OC 1st NFRE

1247 W 3299 200,000 (E) 8/14 J.B.C.&A. Forms/C. 2118/II.

WAR DIARY
or
INTELLIGENCE SUMMARY

(Erase heading not required.)

Army Form C. 2118.

Instructions regarding War Diaries and Intelligence Summaries are contained in F. S. Regs., Part II. and the Staff Manual respectively. Title pages will be prepared in manuscript.

Hour, Date, Place	Summary of Events and Information	Remarks and references to Appendices
YPRES 13/2/15	No. 1086 Sapper G.B. Bone killed in trenches whilst at work on the mine. Lt Stowell blew up small house occupied by German snipers.	
16/2/15	Trench Raid at trenches R & S at night. Trenches wounded in work L on own shrapnel. Following also wounded: 677 L/Cpl. H. Thompson, 887 Sapper N. Harding, 1161 Sapper J.W. Caudle, 1538 — J.R. Taylor, 1196 — T. Dodds	
17/2/15	Took Co. up to C Trench to dig. Wounded: No. 529 L/C T. Burn, 1327 Sapper T.W. Mitford, 1263 Sapper F.C. Matheson, 1459 — J.R. Henderson. Killed 1336 Sapper A. Campbell.	
18/2/15	Took party to S Trench. 2nd Lt Stowell slightly wounded. Injured 1316 Sapper W. Speck, 1487 — F. Jordan	
22/2/15	Lt. Gosling attached for duty to the Co.	
23/2/15	Advised that Major Scott as dead (died 23/2/15)	
26/2/15	Lt Hill & 26 miners (Major Norton Griffiths in) arrived	
27/2/15	2nd Lt McKelvie arrived for duty. Lt Bumpot & 2nd Lt Lancaster + 80 men of monmouths arrived	
4/3/15	2nd Lt Lancaster wounded at trench 27. Sapper Ratcliffe wounded also Private Lewis.	

WAR DIARY
or
INTELLIGENCE SUMMARY.
(Erase heading not required.)

Army Form C. 2118.

Instructions regarding War Diaries and Intelligence Summaries are contained in F.S. Regs., Part II. and the Staff Manual respectively. Title pages will be prepared in manuscript.

Hour, Date, Place	Summary of Events and Information	Remarks and references to Appendices
1/3/15 – 6/3/15 VLAMERTINGE	Building Huttments	
7/3/15 VLAMERTINGE	No 3 Section under 2/Lieut W.H. HEDGES left for duty at YPRES	
8/3/15 – 9/3/15 VLAMERTINGE	Building Huttments. 9/3/15 1 Man to Hospital. 1 Man returned from Hospital	
10/3/15	" " 1 Man to Hospital	
11/3/15	" "	
8 a.m. 12/3/15 VLAMERTINGE	Left by March Route for YPRES.	
10 a.m. 12/3/15 YPRES	Billeted in CAVALRY BARRACKS YPRES. Officers 43 RUE LOMBARD. YPRES. 1 Man to Hospital. No 3 Section under 2/Lieut W.H. HEDGES work on Trenches 43-45.	
13/3/15 YPRES	Lieut D.E. GOSLING returned to Duty with draft from 1st NORTHUMBRIAN FIELD Co. No 1 Section advanced Sap from 32A Trench No 2 " continued communication Trench from Trench 29 – Canal. Lieut G. Patterson returned to Duty with Unit from 3rd LONDON FIELD Co.	
14/3/15 YPRES	Unit together with 1st NORTHUMBRIAN and 3rd LONDON FIELD Cos. dug Fire Trench in prolongation of one at N.E. of ST ELOIT. Casualties: 3 Men Wounded. 1 Man Missing. (afterwards reported killed) A party continued sap from 32A – 8 yards & continued Communication Trench to 29 – 9 yards. N.E. of ST ELOIT	
15/3/15 YPRES	Working party continued work on Fire Trench. Casualty 1 wounded.	
16/3/15 YPRES	Working party sapped from Trench 29 – Canal 2 yards & 3 yards on proposed fire Trench guarding approaches Canal Bank to right of Trench 29.	
17/3/15 YPRES	Working party proceeded with work on Communication Trench between 43-45. 1 Man to Hospital.	

S.C. Tonkes, Major, R.E.
O.C. 1st North Mid. Fd. Co. R.E.

WAR DIARY or INTELLIGENCE SUMMARY

Army Form C. 2118.

Hour, Date, Place	Summary of Events and Information	Remarks and references to Appendices
18-3-1915 YPRES	Working party continued sap 43-45 17 feet. " " " 29 9 feet " " commenced 32 A 6 feet. 3 Men rejoined Unit from Hospital.	
19-3-1915 YPRES	Working party continued Sap 43-45 further 17 feet " " " 29 " 6 feet " " " 32 A " 10 feet 1 Man to Hospital.	
20-3-1915 YPRES	Working party continued Sap 32 A " 10 feet " " " 29 " 3 feet & deepened. " " " 43-45 " 16 feet	
21-3-1915 YPRES	" " " 43-45 " 9 feet " " converted 20 yards Communication Trench to 49 into Fire Trench	
22-3-1915 YPRES	" " continued Sap 43-45 further 12 feet, placed 300 sand bags in position & fixed loophole plate. 1 Man to Hospital	
23-3-1915 YPRES.	Working party made Officers Dug Out rear of 49-50 & commenced 2 Other Dug Outs. " " 3 Loop Holes Trench 33 & fixed 4 Iron Knife Rest Entanglements " " connected Sap 43-45 2 Men to Hospital	
24-3-1915 YPRES	Working party made 10 Iron Knife Rest Entanglements Trench 35 " " completed 1 Dug Out rear 49-50 & half completed another. " " completed Sap 43-45 made loophole & started revetting.	
25-3-1915 YPRES	" " made 6 Iron Knife Rest Entanglements 35 - 36.	

Major, R.E.
O.C. 1st North Mid. Fd. Co. R.E.

28th Division   121/5294

1st Northumbrian Field Coy. RE.

Vol II   5.3 — 30.4.15

NORTHUMBRIAN

WAR DIARY
or
INTELLIGENCE SUMMARY
(Erase heading not required.)

Army Form C. 2118.

Instructions regarding War Diaries and Intelligence Summaries are contained in F. S. Regs., Part II. and the Staff Manual respectively. Title pages will be prepared in manuscript.

Hour, Date, Place	Summary of Events and Information	Remarks and references to Appendices
5/3/15 Ypres	Lt White wounded on night 4/5. Died on 5th at 5 p.m. Joan Hospital at 5 p.m.	
6/3/15	Buried Lt White in ramparts. 2nd Lt Burrell joined from home.	
7/3/15	Sergt Woods killed at no. 27 trench & buried there.	
8/3/15	Sapper Hawley wounded, sent to hospital. Nothing of any interest. Work in trenches as usual.	
9/3/15	Sapper ____ returned to duty from hospital.	
10/3/15	Sapper Hull wounded at canal bank. Lt Gosling rejoined his own company (North Midland R.E.).	
13/3/15	2 (2nd Lt) Taylor H. shot through leg at new trench on St Eloi Road. Rifleman D. Howells (1/1st Monmouths) wounded at same place. Private R J _____ (1/3rd do.) do.	
15/3/15		
16/3/15	Sapper J. Landers shot at trench on St Eloi Rd & died soon after arrival at Rendall château.	
19/3/15	Lt Burnyeat (1/1st Monmouths) shot through leg in Zillebeke village whilst returning from mines.	
26/3/15	Detachment of 1/1st & 1/3rd Monmouths & travelling cookers transferred to 171st Field Co. R.E.	
March - General.	Company employed on trenches & mines. Work on whole getting easier owing to ____ . Have good friends and worked well.	

1247 W 3299 200,000 (E) 8/14 J.B.C. & A. Forms C. 2118/II.

WAR DIARY
or
INTELLIGENCE SUMMARY
(Erase heading not required.)

Army Form C. 2118.

Instructions regarding War Diaries and Intelligence Summaries are contained in F. S. Regs., Part II. and the Staff Manual respectively. Title pages will be prepared in manuscript.

Hour, Date, Place	Summary of Events and Information	Remarks and references to Appendices
April 1st 1915	4th Siege Co. 1st N.M.R.E. (1 Officer (Lt Hill) & 50 N.C.O's & men) attached to Company for work. At work on dugouts behind 32 B.	
2nd	At work on canal bank & dugouts 32 B.	
3rd	4th N.M.R.E. rejoined their own unit. Took my own men to 29 trench. Built 2 dugouts.	
4th	Company went to VLAMERTINGHE & billetted at Suffice Village. Shelled immediately after arrival. I stayed behind to show 59th Co R.E. our work. Stores shifted from Lille Gate to Saw mill.	
5th	Went round right sector with Major White & 3 of his Officers. Joined Company in afternoon.	
6th	Moved to farm H1a (B28). Sawmill Coy working as usual.	
10th	Company returned to Ypres & Billeted in Rue de Seminaire.	
11th	1 & 3 Sections to trenches in Polygon Wood.	
12th	2nd Corporal, 2 Sappers, 1 Driver attached to ASC.	
13th	2/Lt McAloon - 10614 II Corpl Twadlie slightly wounded but remained on duty.	
14th	2 & 4 sections relieved 1 & 3 sections in trenches.	
17th	Bombardment of Hill 60.	

[signature]
1st N.R.E.

WAR DIARY
or
INTELLIGENCE SUMMARY
(Erase heading not required.)

Army Form C. 2118.

Instructions regarding War Diaries and Intelligence Summaries are contained in F. S. Regs., Part II. and the Staff Manual respectively. Title pages will be prepared in manuscript.

Hour, Date, Place	Summary of Events and Information	Remarks and references to Appendices
19/4/15 Ypres	9.4 Sapper J. McKown wounded in trenches.	
	10.75 W.W. Fairless do	
	18.5 H. Bowles do	
20/4/15	Lt Burnell returned to Co. from 171st Co. R.E. Ypres shelled.	
21	Moved out at 6 a.m. to point I 3 C 2.8 & built dugouts.	
	Ypres badly shelled & burnt.	
22	7.90 Sapper A. Herr wounded at sawmill. Shelling continued.	
	Lt McKiver to trenches with relief. Battle north. Gas used by Germans.	
	Transport sent back to Poperinghe.	
23	4.25 Sapper J. Lyon killed at trenches. Burial nr road Polygon Wood.	
24	Transport back from depot. Burial of Spr McKiver. Reliefs as usual.	
	Transport sent back to Mud Farm.	
25	Work in trenches as usual. Ypres shelled every day. All work through	
26	as usual.	
27-30	Men well & in good spirits, though not recovered the first shock	
	of bombardment for some days when shell fire day & night.	
	[signature]	

28th Division

121/5356

1st Northumbrian Field Coy: RE

Vol III 1 — 31. 5. 15.

WAR DIARY or INTELLIGENCE SUMMARY

Army Form C. 2118.

Instructions regarding War Diaries and Intelligence Summaries are contained in F. S. Regs., Part II. and the Staff Manual respectively. Title pages will be prepared in manuscript.

(Erase heading not required.)

1st Northumbrian Field Co. R.E.

Hour, Date, Place	Summary of Events and Information	Remarks and references to Appendices
1st May 1915 — YPRES.	Sapper Ballantyne (No. 1459) wounded at trenches — Polygon Wood.	
2	Another attack — YPRES. Gas used. Heavy shelling.	
3/5	Lieut Wickham C. [?] [?], moved Company to H.12.c.8.6. Stonall, Bunnell & party came back.	
4/5	Cpl Wardine (1083) killed on road & Sergt Mitchell (769) wounded by shell whilst going to Bryd. H.Q. and me. At work at night with Stonall — 30 men on trench from St Jean X Rds to Turco Wood. Heavy shelling. Brigade H.Q. transferred from Canvas to their dugout to one dugout at St Jean	
5/5 6/5 7/5	Improved dugouts at Brigade H.Q. Lt. Stonall back to Billbrook. Reconnoitred G.H.Q. line S. of Potize with Major Morris.	
8/5	New trench Potize — St Jean. Heavy shelling. Capt. Bunnell back to C.	
9/5	Party at St Jean with Bunnell & McElvire wiring new trench. Bunnell sick of influenza, gone to Canvas, infm.	
10/5	Returned support points Potize — Railway. Arrangts for hogsheads, Col James sick Major Brown CRE (acting). Support points constructed.	
11/5 12/5 13/5	Bunnell party to trenches. Water reconnce with Major McHardy Canvas shelled out. New trench in rear of support points.	

G. Willand
Major

WAR DIARY or **INTELLIGENCE SUMMARY**

Army Form C. 2118.

Instructions regarding War Diaries and Intelligence Summaries are contained in F. S. Regs., Part II. and the Staff Manual respectively. Title pages will be prepared in manuscript.

(Erase heading not required.)

1st Northumbrian Field Co. R.E.

Hour, Date, Place	Summary of Events and Information	Remarks and references to Appendices
16/5/15 YPRES	Inspected Canal Line with General Glubb & Petrie.	
17 – 21	Busy on Canal line. While working with Anglesea Co. a 400–500 Belgians Refugees passed along us. Good progress made. Weather dull. Few planes. Handed over on night of 21–22 to Field Squadron (Major Johnson).	
22/5/15	Attached 8.3 Bde (Cavalry Corps). Saw Brigadier Rawlinson. Took over from 2nd Wessex R.E.	
23/5/15	Saw Major Sandys (CRE Cavalry Corps). Went up to line N of ZILLEBEKE. Lieut Burrup, Russell & 3 Section of it with for 4 days. At work on Reserve line & Support posts.	
24/5/15	Heavy attack N & NE of YPRES. Gas very bad. R.H.A. in our billet is moved to woodyard at Vlamertinghe. Took 1 & 2 section to Zouave Wood, digging & wiring. Heavy rifle fire when Germans have broken through near HOOGE.	
25	At work in woodyard. Went up myself to see Burrup at trenches. Col. Winslow CRE	
26	Party on water supply, H.1.a. Stovell out at night to prepare support points near of line. Sergt Wordhouse sent to hospital.	
27	To trenches at night. Stovell & party relieved Burrell. At work on Support posts & reserve line.	
28	Mr. Lantjan to CRE. Lt. Paton back from HILLHOEK. 2 sections at work in trench stores. Major Soper (17 Co. RE) relieves Major Sandys.	
29	McKelvie to trenches. Capt. Burrup took 5 A.L.	
30	To trenches at night. Sited position for another Support post & inspected work done.	
31	A. Stovell to hospital (neuralgia). Paid in/c at VLAMERTINGHE. Capt. Burrup & No. 2 Company R.E. Burgel & relief party to trenches. Paid party to Hillhoek.	

1247 W 3299 200,000 (E) 8/14 J.B.C.&A. Forms/C. 2118/11.

R. Pollard
1st N R.E.

WO95/2272(3)

WO95/2272(3)

REF

28 DIV TROON
2/1 NORTHUMBRIAN FLD OY RE
1915 JLY — 1915 OCT

To SALONIKA

WAR DIARY or INTELLIGENCE SUMMARY

Army Form C. 2118.

Volume 1

Place	Date	Hour	Summary of Events and Information	Remarks and references to Appendices
England	3/4/15	Midnight	Marched out of Camp at Southwell for Farnsfield Station where Company entrained. Train left 2.55 A.M. Arrived Southampton 2.0 p.m. Embarked on S.S. "Chyebassa" of Glasgow. Sailed 5.0 p.m.	
France Le Havre	4/7/15	2.0 AM 6.0 AM	Arrived. Disembarked and marched to No 5 Rest Camp	
	5/7/15	2.0 pm	Marched out of Rest Camp to station. Entrained. Train started 5.0 pm	
	6/7/15	3.0 pm	Arrived at Bailleul - disentrained and marched to St. Jans Capelle where bivouaced.	
	8-9/7/15		St. Jans Capelle	
	10/7/15		Left St. Jans Capelle at 6.0 pm. Marched to Locre arriving 10.0 pm. No 1, 2, 3 and 4 sections Cyclists proceeded to R.E. Farm, Kemmel. G1 Mine blown up by Germans.	

WAR DIARY
or
INTELLIGENCE SUMMARY.

(Erase heading not required.)

Army Form C. 2118.

Instructions regarding War Diaries and Intelligence Summaries are contained in F. S. Regs., Part II. and the Staff Manual respectively. Title pages will be prepared in manuscript.

2nd/1st NORTHUMBRIAN FIELD COY. R.E. (T.F.)

Place	Date	Hour	Summary of Events and Information	Remarks and references to Appendices
Kemmel	14/7/15		Sapper G. Graham Wounded	
	15/7/15		II Lieut. Needham surveyed subsidiary line, Kemmel	

W.H. Shipp

WAR DIARY
or
INTELLIGENCE SUMMARY.
(Erase heading not required.)

Army Form C. 2118.

Instructions regarding War Diaries and Intelligence Summaries are contained in F. S. Regs., Part II. and the Staff Manual respectively. Title pages will be prepared in manuscript.

Volume I(A)

2nd/1st NORTHUMBRIAN FIELD COY. R.E. (T.F.)

Place	Date	Hour	Summary of Events and Information	Remarks and references to Appendices
Kemmel	4/8/15		Working Party in L' Trench stopped by Shelling	
	18/8/15		Mine in G' exploded by British	
	25/8/15		Mine opposite J3 New exploded by Germans	
	26/8/15		Lieut. G. K. Walker wounded at Sandbag Villa. Shot in leg.	
	28/8/15		Lieut. G. K. Walker discharged from Hospital but not fit for duty.	

WH Tripp Lt RE

WAR DIARY or INTELLIGENCE SUMMARY

2/1. Northumbrian Fd Coy RE
Volume I (B)
Army Form C. 2118.

Place	Date	Hour	Summary of Events and Information	Remarks and references to Appendices
Kemmel	3/9/15		H.Q. and No 1 Section removed to Brewery in Locre	
	4/9/15		H.Q and No 1 " back to original billets in Locre	
	9/9/15		Mine in D4 trench exploded by II Lieut C.P. Gordon	
			H.Qrs and No 2 Section removed to Locre Hof Farm	
	11/9/15		Working parties stopped by shelling in Fosse. H.Qrs and No 3 Section left Locre Hof for billet near Kemmel	
	21/9/15		All men at R.E. Farm, Kemmel removed to H.Qrs in farm about 2 miles off.	
	22/9/15		Marched via Bailleul, Strazeele to Pradelles	
	25/9/15		Standing by.	
	26/9/15		Marched from Pradelles 8.0 am to Merville to Rieg du Vinage. Bivouaced for night.	
	27/9/15		Marched via Bethune to Vermelles and bivouaced at 10.0 pm	
	28/9/15	12.30 AM	Sappers out to dig. 2.0 pm - moved back ½ mile to Philosoph & bivouaced	
	29/9/15		Lieut. Forster killed about 11.0 pm. Company out cutting firing steps in West Face Hohenzollern Redoubt.	
	30/9/15		Lieut. Forster buried at Vermelles.	

WHSLipps
Locre

WAR DIARY or INTELLIGENCE SUMMARY

2/1 Northumbrian Field Cy RE
28° Div
Volume I (c)

Army Form C. 2118.

(Erase heading not required.)

2nd/1st NORTHUMBRIAN FIELD COY. R.E.

Place	Date	Hour	Summary of Events and Information	Remarks and references to Appendices
Vermelles	1-2/10/15		Working at Night.	
	3/10/15	7.30pm	3 horses killed by shell at Philosoph	
	6/10/15	2.0am	Sapper Redshaw wounded. 11.30 AM - Left Philosoph via Bethune, Chocques and Burnes to Berguette and billetted.	
	8/10/15		Inspection by General Sir D. Haig.	
	9/10/15		Sitting Board of Officers.	
	11/10/15		Marched from Berguette 9.30 am for Bethune and billetted. Lieut Rain joined Unit. Billetted - Faubourg d'Arras.	
	12/10/15		Company out digging new fire trench between Burberry Alley and Wilsons Way, Cambrin	
	13/10/15		Bethune shelled.	
	14-16/10/15		Working on new trenches.	
	17/10/15		Left for Cambrin and billetted No 4 Harley St. H.Qrs remain at Bethune.	
	21/10/15	8.0am	Marched from Cambrin. Arrived Gonnehem at 2.0 pm and billetted.	
	23/10/15	12.0pm	Marched to Lillers and entrained. Train left 7.5 am.	
	25/10/15		Arrived Marseilles 1.30 pm and marched to Parc Borely and encamped	

W.H.S. Tripp Lt.R.E

www.ingramcontent.com/pod-product-compliance
Lightning Source LLC
Chambersburg PA
CBHW081251170426
43191CB00037B/2113